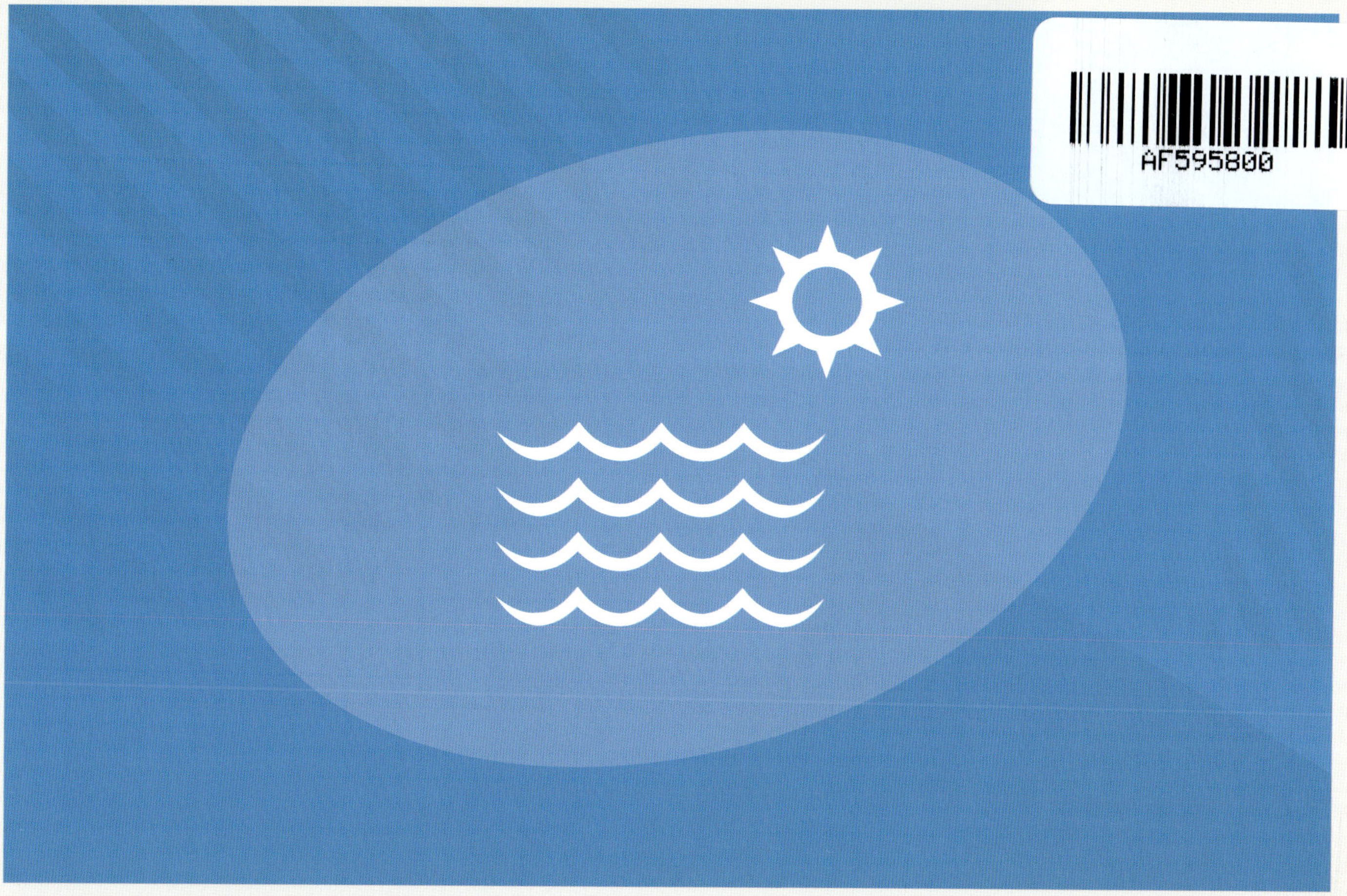

Australia's Environmental Issues

WATER

Redback Publishing
PO Box 357 Frenchs Forest NSW 2086
Australia

www.redbackpublishing.com.au
orders@redbackpublishing.com.au

978-1-925860-31-3

Author: Peter Turner
Editor: Michael Anderson
Proofer: Marianne Lindsell
Designer: Redback Publishing

MIX
Paper from responsible sources
FSC® C020056
FSC www.fsc.org

Original illustrations © Redback Publishing 2019
Originated by Redback Publishing

Printed and bound in China by Leo Paper

Acknowledgements
Abbreviations: l—left, r—right, b—bottom, t—top, c—centre, m—middle
We would like to thank the following for permission to reproduce photographs: (Images © shutterstock) p13b Antonov14 via Wikimedia, p14m Aboriginal Australian woman fishing from a canoe, State Library of Queensland, p15 The rainbow serpent by Winam @ flickr

Every effort has been made to contact copyright holders of any material reproduced in this book. Any omissions will be rectified in subsequent printings if notice is given to the publisher.

Disclaimer
All the internet addresses (URLs) given in this book were valid at the time of going to press. However, due to the dynamic nature of the internet, some addresses may have changed, or sites may have changed or ceased to exist since publication. While the author and publisher regret any inconvenience this may cause readers, no responsibility for any such changes can be accepted by either the author or the publisher.

NATIONAL LIBRARY OF AUSTRALIA
A catalogue record for this book is available from the National Library of Australia

CONTENTS

INTRODUCTION:
WHY IS WATER IMPORTANT?

Water is one of the essential building blocks of life. Much of our planet is covered in water. Plants need water to survive and grow, and so do animals, including ourselves. Humans are made up of more than 70 per cent water, and we all need to consume around 2 litres of water a day. Water is also used in industry, agriculture and many other areas of our lives. It is the most important resource on the planet.

The History of Water

It is extraordinary to think that the water supplied through our taps today has been around since Earth came into existence 4.6 billion years ago. The same water that fills our oceans, lakes and rivers falls from the sky as rain and comes out of our taps. Water may change from and move around - from freshwater on land to water vapour in the atmosphere, to rain falling from clouds, to salt water in the ocean - but it is essentially the same water. This means that we have a limited supply of water. No more will ever be created, so we must use it responsibly.

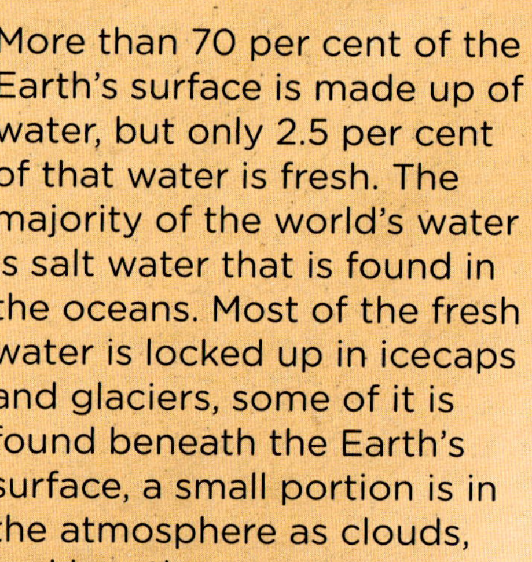

GLOBAL WATER

More than 70 per cent of the Earth's surface is made up of water, but only 2.5 per cent of that water is fresh. The majority of the world's water is salt water that is found in the oceans. Most of the fresh water is locked up in icecaps and glaciers, some of it is found beneath the Earth's surface, a small portion is in the atmosphere as clouds, and less than one per cent fills rivers and lakes.

WATER IN AUSTRALIA

Differences in weather patterns and landscapes mean that some countries receive more rain and have more water on land than others. For example, England receives a great deal of water in the form of rain, sleet and snow. Consequently, it has a lush, green landscape with plants that grow quickly. In contrast, Australia is a very dry continent with minimal rainfall, particularly in the centre and south of the country. Two-thirds of Australia is arid or semi-arid, which means that rainfall is extremely low.

DROUGHT

Australia is prone to drought, which is a long period of below-average rainfall. Droughts can affect a farmers' ability to grow crops and feed their livestock. They can also affect people in towns and cities, and from time to time they may be asked to adhere to water restrictions and to conserve water as much as possible. In addition, most of our inland rivers dry up during summer months, making it more difficult to obtain a regular supply of water.

FAST FACT

WE CAN SURVIVE FOR UP TO A MONTH WITHOUT FOOD, BUT ONLY ABOUT THREE DAYS WITHOUT WATER.

CLIMATE CHANGE AND WATER

Climate change is the process by which the overall average temperature around the world changes from one average to a new average. Currently, we are experiencing a period of rapid global warming. The overall average temperature has increased by nearly one degree in the past 60 years and it is expected to increase further. This will dramatically affect the distribution of water on Earth. Rainfall patterns are expected to change. Some countries will experience heavier rainfall and violent storms. Others, such as Australia, will have much less rainfall. When it does rain, it may be extreme and sudden, resulting in flooding. The lack of consistent rainfall may affect our ability to grow crops and farm livestock, and bushfires will become an increasingly persistent problem.

DISTURBING FACTS ABOUT WATER....

1. Australians use 13 billion plastic drink containers annually.

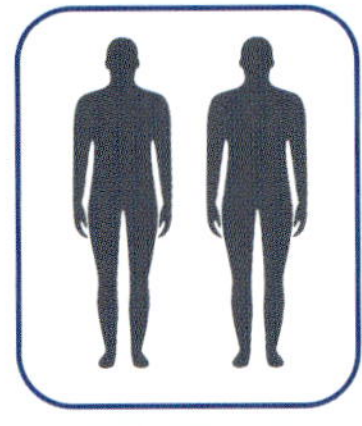

2. Every Australian resident uses an average of 341,000 litres of water per year.

3. The most polluted river in Australia is the King River in Tasmania.

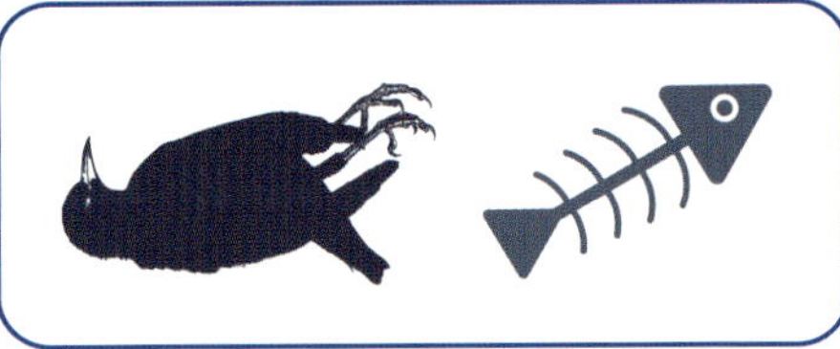

4. 50 to 80 per cent of wetlands in the Murray-Darling Basin have been severely damaged or completely destroyed.

5. One "sydharb" is the amount of water in Sydney Harbour: approximately 500 gigalitres. This unit of volume is used in Australia to describe the amount of water in large water bodies such as lakes and dams.

6. Australia is the highest user of water per person in the world, despite being the driest inhabited continent.

7. Australia's largest water storage is Lake Pedder (TAS) which stores 12,450 gigalitres.

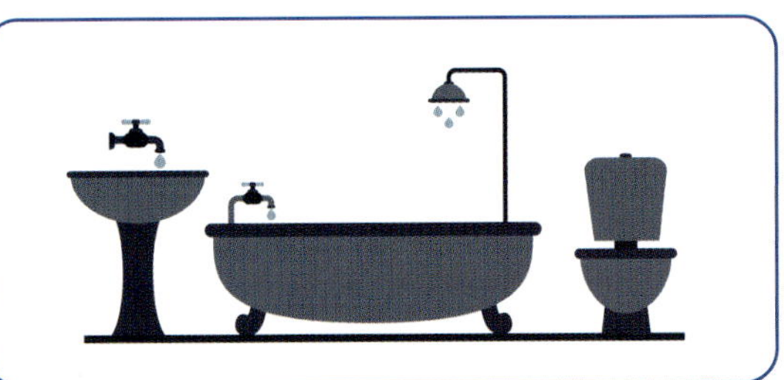

8. Average household consumption in Melbourne is 240,000 litres per year, or 5 swimming pools.

1. By 2015, 3.5 billion people will suffer a water shortage.

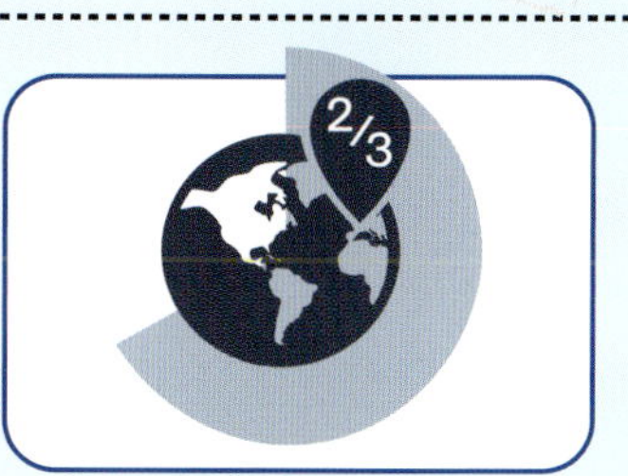

3. By 2025, water will be scarce for two-thirds of the world.

2. Global water demands will increase by 40 per cent in the next 10 years.

4. Three per cent of all deaths worldwide are related to water safety.

5. 15 million children die annually due to unsafe or inadequate water.

6. Every day, 2 million tonnes of human waste and pollution makes its way into the world's water systems.

8. More than two billion people worldwide rely on wells for their water.

7. Two-thirds of Chinese cities already suffer from water shortages.

USING WATER

Besides the water we use every day in the kitchen, bathroom and laundry, water is consumed in many ways that we do not see. A huge amount of water is used on farms, to irrigate crops and as drinking water for livestock such as cattle and sheep. Water is also used in large quantities to produce the energy to run lights, heaters and other appliances in our homes. Likewise, water is used to manufacture many everyday products, such as soap and shampoo. We need water in many vital areas of our lives. Without it, our society could not function.

Households

At home, we use the largest amount of water in the bathroom, flushing the toilet and taking showers. We use a lot of water outdoors, on our gardens, washing the car and perhaps filling the pool. The average Australian households consumes up to 300,000 litres of water every year. When you factor in all the food we eat and the water that goes into the products we buy, it is estimated we each use about one million litres of water a year. That's enough water to fill Sydney Harbour 48 times over!

ELECTRICITY

Hydro-electricity uses the power of moving water to generate electricity. Hydro power plants located on the water channels, where they harness the power of moving water to turn large turbines or windmills that are hooked up to an alternator, which produces electricity. In Australia, we have 55 hydropower stations with a total capacity of 7,600 megawatts of electricity. Most of our hydro-electricity comes from the Snowy Mountains Hydro Scheme and the Tasmanian Hydroelectric Corporation. Many coal-fired power plants also use water in the process of generating electricity.

AGRICULTURE

Agriculture, or growing crops and caring for livestock, is responsible for more than 70 per cent of total water usage in Australia. Many crops need to be watered regularly, so rainfall needs to be supplemented with irrigation. This is very expensive and uses enormous amounts of water from dams and rivers. Four crops consume the majority of the world's agricultural water and they are all grown in Australia. They are cotton, rice, sugar cane and wheat.

INDUSTRY

The manufacturing of products is responsible for three per cent of Australia's total water usage. Mining also uses three per cent. The hospitality industry – including restaurants, cafes and catering companies – uses large amounts of water in cleaning food and washing dishes. Hotels use an enormous amount of water. A 300-room hotel uses up to 1.3 Olympic swimming pools of water every day just keeping things clean.

The Snowy Mountains Hydro Scheme

Australia's largest hydro-electric power plant is the Snowy Mountains Hydro Scheme in southern New South Wales, which generates 50 per cent of our total hydropower. It is made up of 16 large dams and underground water sources high in the Snowy Mountains. The largest dam, on Lake Eucumbene, holds nine times more than Sydney Harbour. The scheme collects and stores water that would otherwise flow downstream. The water flows through giant turbines, creating electricity that then travels through cables to our homes and business.

FAST FACT

AUSTRALIA IS THE DRIEST INHABITED CONTINENT ON THE PLANET, WITH MORE THAN 70 PER CENT OF OUR LAND CONSISTING OF DESERT OR SEMI-DESERT, AND YET WE ARE ONE OF THE BIGGEST CONSUMERS PER PERSON OF WATER ON EARTH.

PROVIDING WATER

Our need for water in so many areas of our lives means that we cannot rely solely on the water that falls as rain. We must also obtain water from lakes, rivers and even underground sources. However, using water from these other sources has an impact on natural water flows and the wildlife that may need them to survive.

Dams and Reservoirs

In Australia, we store nearly four million litres of water per person in dams and reservoirs, which are large water-storage areas. These help to compensate for the variability in rainfall throughout the year, ensuring that in dry seasons, such as summer, we have sufficient water. Dams help keep towns and cities supplied with water, provide irrigation for agriculture and even help to provide electricity via hydroelectric power stations. There are around 450 large dams, as well as millions of small dams on farms, throughout Australia.

RIVERS

Australia has many important rivers that provide water to farms and townships in the dry interior of the continent. But when the paths of rivers are changed to provide water for irrigation, plants and animals may lose their water source, and other environmental problems may be created. Barriers known as weirs, which prevent the water from flowing downriver, block the natural flow of some rivers. Weirs also stop a river from flooding every few years, which is a natural occurrence that rejuvenates plant species along the riverbank. Some Australian rivers have stopped flowing in summer partly because of the impact of these changes.

GREAT ARTESIAN BASIN

Around 80 per cent of Australia's land is dependent on water that lies beneath the ground. One-third of this ground water is fresh, while the rest is too salty for human use. Much of our groundwater comes from the Great Artesian Basin, which covers around 1.7 million square kilometres, making it one of the largest areas of underground water in the world. The basin is mainly in Queensland, with smaller segments in New South Wales, South Australia and the Northern Territory.

The water in the basin is sometimes referred to as 'dinosaur water' because it is believed to be almost 2 million years old. It is accessed through bores, which are large pipes drilled into the ground. The pressure of the water pushes it up to the surface, or sometimes it is pumped up. There are more than 18,000 boreholes, which take more than 1,500 megalitres of water from the basin every day.

FAST FACT

AUSTRALIA'S THREE LONGEST RIVERS ARE ALL PART OF THE MURRAY-DARLING BASIN: THE DARLING (2,740 KILOMETRES), MURRAY (2,530 KILOMETRES) AND MURRUMBIDGEE RIVERS (1,690 KILOMETRES).

The Murray-Darling River Basin

This important area of rivers covers 14 per cent of Australia's total land mass and spans five states. Its waters are used in more than 40 per cent of our agricultural production and satisfy more than 70 per cent of our irrigation needs.

The basin encompasses the Murray River and the Darling River, as well as the many smaller rivers that flow from them. There are also many dams and major water storage areas throughout the basin, where water can be stored during wet periods for use in dry periods. However, changing the landscape has reduced the number of plant and animal species, drastically reduced the flow of some rivers, and many of the original water springs have dried up. A program is now being undertaken to restore the flows of the Murray-Darling River Basin.

THE WATER CYCLE

The water on Earth is constantly moving and changing its form - this process is called the water cycle. When rain falls, it soaks into the ground and adds to the groundwater or becomes part of lakes, rivers and oceans. Some rainwater evaporates and eventually becomes rain again.

Evaporation and Transpiration

Evaporation is the process by which water transforms into a vapour, such as when you boil the kettle and steam comes out of the spout. Evaporation in nature occurs when the sun hits water on the land or ocean surface. The heat turns the water into an invisible gas or vapour, which then travels up into the atmosphere to become part of the clouds. Transpiration is the process by which leaves of plants release the water they have absorbed as vapour into the atmosphere. Both evaporation and transpiration are essential parts of the water cycle - without them, we would not have any rain!

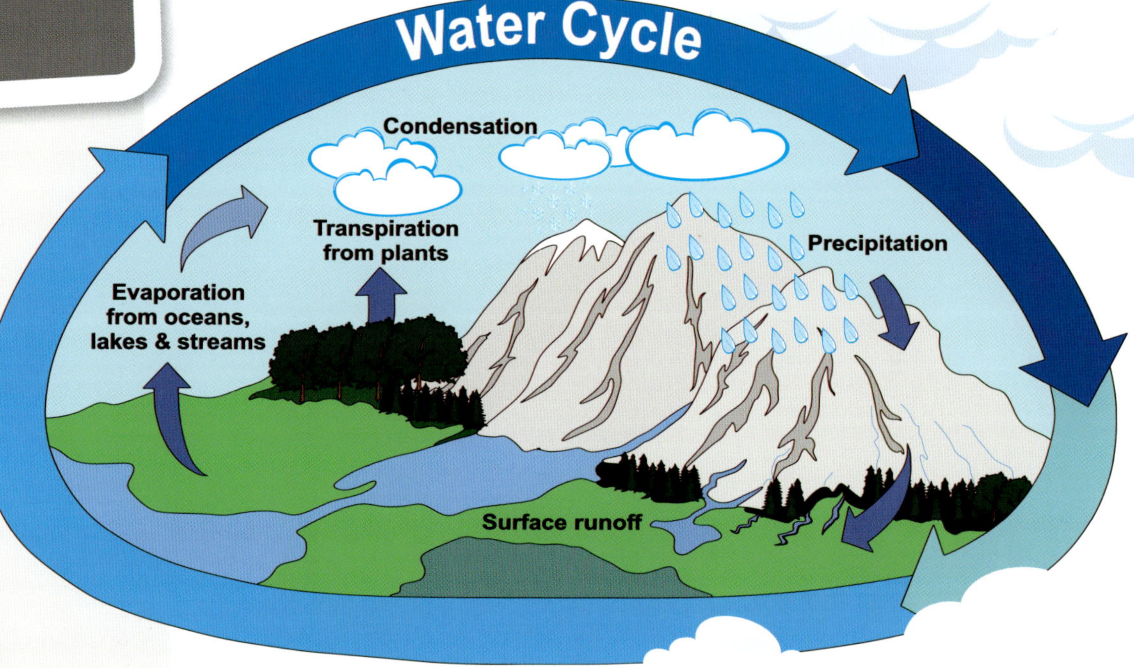

Rainfall

Australia receives very little rainfall, with 80 per cent of the land receiving less than 60 centimetres of rain a year and 50 per cent receiving less than 30 centimetres a year. So, half of Australia gets less than half a bathtub of water over a whole year! In general, inland areas receive very little rain, which is one of the reasons why Australia's population is concentrated in high-rainfall coastal areas where it is easier to grow crops and supply households with water. The area with the lowest rainfall is Lake Eyre in South Australia, with only 10 centimetres of rain a year. In contrast, Happy Valley on the east coast of Queensland receives a whopping 4.5 metres a year.

CLOUDS

Evaporated water, or water vapour, cools and expands as it rises in the atmosphere. Cool air cannot hold as much as water vapour as warm air, so some of the vapour forms around dust particles and becomes tiny water droplets. Billions of these particles form clouds, which are really just a large collection of water droplets or ice crystals. The clouds move on wind currents, sometimes travelling at more than 100 kilometres an hour. Eventually, when the air temperature or air pressure falls, the water falls from the clouds as rain.

RUNOFF WATER

On average, only 12 per cent of rainfall becomes part of rivers, streams and lakes, either by running off the land or falling directly into them. In tropical areas, the ground is already damp so more water runs off, whereas in dry areas the opposite occurs and there is very little runoff. Sometimes, the runoff water seeps into the ground to become groundwater.

EL NIÑO AND LA NIÑA

El Niño is a weather pattern that results in the warming of air and water along the coast of South America and eventually down to Australia. It occurs every three to seven years and has many consequences for the world's climate and water cycles. In Australia, an El Niño period usually results in less rain and more drought conditions, which reduces the overall water supply. The 1982-1983 El Niño was one of the worst on record. It caused massive landslides and floods in the USA and droughts in Australia, Indonesia and south-east Africa. La Niña is the reverse of the El Niño pattern and in Australia it tends to bring more wet weather.

FAST FACT

AROUND 88 PER CENT OF AUSTRALIA'S ANNUAL RAINFALL IS RETURNED TO THE ATMOSPHERE THROUGH EVAPORATION AND TRANSPIRATION.

WATER OVER TIME

Water has existed on Earth for 4.6 billion years, which is far longer than humans. Without water, plants, animals and we humans would not exist. The water on the planet has shifted and changed over time. During the ice ages, the majority of water was locked in glaciers and ice sheets. At other times, the planet was much wetter, with rain and running water in abundance.

Water in the Past

Australia has seen many variations in climate and water. Until about 11,000 years ago, Tasmania was joined to the Australian mainland by a land bridge. There were once huge lakes in the centre of the country. Scientists believe Australia experienced more rainfall between 9,000 and 3,500 years ago and that there may have been many more tropical cyclones and severe floods. Evidence gathered from trees in Tasmania suggests that the climate has changed a great deal in the past 3,000 years, with an increase in temperature.

INDIGENOUS PEOPLE AND WATER

Aboriginal people have lived in Australia for more than 60,000 years and have experienced many changes in the country's climate and landscape. However, they have always understood the importance of conserving water in dry areas. Certain places were not used except in times of extreme drought, in order to protect the plants and animals. There were also rules to protect rivers and waterholes. Fish were a very important food source for many clans, particularly along the coast. Indigenous people sometimes built dams to trap large fish, while allowing small ones to survive and breed. Evidence of ancient fish traps has been found near Coffs Harbour and on the Darling River at Brewarrina in New South Wales. Indigenous people valued water and understood that, if their food sources were to last, they needed to be looked after.

WATER IN FUTURE

It is predicted that climate change will have an enormous impact on Australia's water supplies in the coming century. While areas in the north of the country will experience increased rainfall and periods of severe flooding, in the west and south there will probably be far less water and more extreme droughts. As the temperature rises, more water will evaporate into the air, reducing the flow of water in rivers and water availability over all.

Ancient Tales

Water is present in ancient stories and myths from almost every culture. It represents the source of life, purity of spirit and feminine energy.

The Rainbow Serpent

The Rainbow Serpent is a large, snake like creature that is associated with rivers, creeks and billabongs in Aboriginal mythology. It is an all powerful protector of the land and the people, and is depicted in rock art some 6000 years old. The origins of the Rainbow Serpent vary across Indigenous peoples. Some say it came over the sea with their ancestors inside, while others say it came from the ground, creating mountains and gorges as it pushed its way up to the surface.

IRRIGATION

Many plants require irrigation, or watering above and beyond rainfall, in order to grow. Without irrigation, Australia's agricultural industry would not be nearly as productive as it is.

Why Irrigate?

Many areas of Australia are so dry that crops would not be able to grow without the extra water they receive from irrigation. In order to produce our own food and other products, we need to irrigate. Agriculture uses huge amounts of irrigated water to grow crops, including wheat, fruit and vegetables, cotton and flowers. But some crops use far more than others. For example, more than 90 per cent of Australia's cotton is grown using irrigation, using up to 12 per cent of our total irrigated water. Most cotton is grown in New South Wales and Queensland.

HOW IRRIGATION WORKS

Irrigation systems usually consist a series of pipes, furrows or sprinklers that distribute the water from the main water supply to the plants that need it. In a process called furrow irrigation, large channels or furrows are dug between crops, such as grapevines. The water is directed through these channels to irrigate the soil. Orchards may be flooded with large amounts of water, completely soaking the soil. This irrigation method takes a great deal of water, up to 70 per cent of which may seep away or evaporate. Many farmers now use drip irrigation, which is the most efficient way of watering crops. The water is slowly dripped directly into the soil around the roots of the plants. This prevents evaporation, or the loss of water to the atmosphere.

Irrigation and the Murray River

The Murray River, which forms the boundary between New South Wales and Victoria, is a vital source of water for irrigation for many farmers. In the 1920s, around 15 per cent of the river's water was used for irrigation, but by 2001 this figure had risen to 80 per cent. This has had a huge impact on the water flow, as well as on the animals and plants that depend on the river. In particular, many fish are now unable to swim downriver because of the dams and weirs that capture water for irrigation. Some fish that used to be plentiful, such as the famous Murray River Cod, have almost disappeared in the wild due to excessive irrigation. Scientists are now working on restoring the flow of the Murray River.

PROBLEMS

Excessive irrigation over time can cause soil to become very salty. This happens because all water other than rainwater contains salt. While seawater contains the highest level of salt, even water from rivers and dams contains some salt. When plants absorb the water, they leave the salt behind in the soil. It slowly builds up, causing a problem called salinity. Eventually, the soil may become too salty for crops to grow. Another problem is over-watering crops, particularly when using the flooding method of irrigation. The roots of plants can become waterlogged, which kills the plants. Technological advances in measuring the exact amount of water needed by crops have helped to make the best use of our limited water supplies.

FOOD AND WATER

A great deal of water goes into producing many of the foods we eat every day. The milk you had on your cereal this morning took around 200 litres of water to produce. If you are having steak for dinner tonight, even more water has been used in getting it to your plate.

Embodied Water

Embodied water, or virtual water, is the amount of water it takes to produce a food or other product. It includes the amount of water a crop needs to grow or that livestock needs to drink, as well as the water used in processing the product. Some products take much more water to produce than others – beef and dairy foods have some of the highest levels of embodied water, whereas vegetables have some of the lowest.

FRUIT AND VEGETABLES

Fruit and vegetable farming, or horticulture, is an important industry in Australia. It currently brings in nearly $6 billion a year in export earnings and is one of our fastest-growing industries. Horticulture is undertaken in a wide variety of climate zones, with most of our fruit and vegetable crops requiring irrigation, although the water is generally used very efficiently. Water levels must be carefully monitored, as over-watering can result in disease and excessive soil salinity.

DAIRY FARMING

The dairy industry uses about 25 per cent of the water allocated to irrigation in Australia. More than 10 billion litres of milk are produced annually, and cows need to be fed on grass that is high in nutrients, and which therefore requires irrigation. Dairy farmers also use water to clean out milking sheds in order to maintain a hygienic environment. Most dairy farming is undertaken in southeast Australia, with 64 per cent of milk produced in Victoria. On average, it takes 1 megalitre (1 million litres) of water to produce 1,200 litres of milk.

Embodied water content of common foods:

- A slice of bread- 40 litres
- An apple- 70 litres
- A 200-gram bag of potato crisps- 185 litres
- An egg- 200 litres
- A 200-millilitre glass of milk- 200 litres
- A 150-gram hamburger- 2,400 litres
- One kilo of rice- 3,400 litres

FAST FACT

AUSTRALIA IS THE WORLD'S FOURTH-LARGEST EXPORTER OF EMBODIED WATER, WHICH IS FOUND IN PRODUCTS SUCH AS DAIRY FOODS, BEEF, RICE AND COTTON.

RICE FARMING

Australia produces more than one million tonnes of rice annually, making it our third-largest cereal export. Rice is grown primarily in the Murrumbidgee Valley and the Murray Valley in New South Wales. It requires more water to grow than any of our other food crops and is mainly flood-irrigated. It takes 1.2 megalitres of water to produce one tonne of rice. Given our scarce water resources, some people believe that rice should not be grown in Australia, but only in countries that have high rainfall, such as Thailand.

POPULATION AND WATER

A country's water needs depend on the size of its population. Large populations require more water, which can strain water resources, particularly in very dry places like Australia. Many countries in the world today have serious water shortages, with growing populations adding to the problem.

Water Infrastructure

The greater the population, the more water is required and the more infrastructure needed to deliver it. In Australia, most household water is taken from dams and weirs, then filtered and cleaned at water treatment plants before travelling through systems of pipelines to our homes. The infrastructure required to clean and deliver water is very expensive, especially in a country as large as Australia. As the population grows, more infrastructure is needed to supply and treat the water required. Without this infrastructure, whole communities would run out of clean, safe water.

MALARIA FACT FILE

Insects that breed in water can also spread diseases including malaria and yellow fever. In 2016:

- 216 million people had malaria worldwide, an increase of five million cases from the previous year.
- 445,000 of those people died.
- 91 per cent of the deaths occurred in Africa.

Unsafe water causes the death of over a million people each year.

A child dies from a water related disease every 90 seconds.

884 million people worldwide live without access to safe water.

THE DEVELOPING WORLD

In many poor countries, the need for water is a daily battle. In rural Africa, women may walk 10 kilometres or more a day to collect water from a well. They carry it home in containers that weigh upwards of 25 kilograms. They may also have to queue for hours at the well before they can fill their containers. To avoid this problem, some get up in the middle of the night to go to the well. In some African countries, it can take more than six hours a day to collect water for a family's needs. Water scarcity remains an urgent global problem, as does water pollution.

WATER THAT KILLS

When in Australia we take pure tap water for granted, elsewhere more than one million people die every year due to poor access to clean water. Many waterborne diseases can be spread through contaminated water, including typhoid, dysentery and cholera. Diarrhoea is often caused by contaminated water and is usually a minor annoyance in most places. However, in developing countries, it can lead to death.

POPULATION GROWTH IN AUSTRALIA

Currently, Australia has a population of more than 20 million people and our water reserves are stretched to the limit. Population growth of 8.5 million people is expected by 2050, which is equivalent to two or more cities the size of Sydney. If we continue to consume water at our current rate and our population does increase by 8.5 million, an extra 1,000 gigalitres of water will be required each year. Right now, we do not have the capacity to provide this water. In Australia, water availability is an urgent problem.

WATER FOOTPRINT

Our water footprint is the amount of water we use as a country. It includes the goods and services consumed, even if these were produced outside the country. Australia's water footprint is 1,393 megalitres (1,393 million litres) per person per year. This is a huge figure and far beyond what we individually consume from the tap. In fact, 18 per cent of that amount is used outside Australia and represents the embodied water in the products we import.

Indigenous People's Water Declaration

At the Third World Water Forum in 2003, at Kyoto, Japan, Indigenous peoples from across the globe signed an international declaration affirming the importance of water in the 21st century. Their declaration stated: We, the Indigenous Peoples from all parts of the world assembled here, reaffirm our relationship to Mother Earth and responsibility to future generations to raise our voices in solidarity to speak for protection of water. We were placed in sacred manner on this earth, each in our own sacred traditional lands and territories to care for creation and to care for water.

CONSERVING WATER

Australia does not have enough water to go around, so we need to make sure we conserve what water we do have. This is already vitally important, but becomes even more urgent in the face of potential water shortages caused by climate change and a growing population.

The Price of Water

Despite its scarcity, Australians regarded water as a free resource for a long time. When something is free, people do not always value it enough. Although we now pay for water, the cost is mainly for treatment and transportation, rather than for the water itself. The price of water still varies a great deal throughout the country, with urban users generally paying more than rural users, such as farmers. In Australia, water is still very cheap compared with other countries around the world, but the price is increasing.

WATER RESTRICTIONS

Most states in Australia are now on some level of water restrictions due to lack of rainfall and low water levels in dams. Restrictions vary from state to state and are often tougher in the dry summer months. Some states, such as Queensland, are on permanent restrictions. At home, restrictions may include watering lawns and gardens only at certain times, or sometimes not at all, and severely restricting any outdoor water usage such as washing the car or filling the pool. At work, people are being asked to reduce their water usage significantly in kitchens and bathrooms. Large businesses that use enormous amounts of water are also being asked to look at how they can conserve water. For example, hotels are being encouraged not to wash guest towels' every day. People who do not comply with water restrictions can be fined.

WATER-RATING LABELS

The National Water Efficiency Labelling and Standards (WELS) Scheme devised a mandatory ratings system for showers, taps, toilets, washing machines and dishwashers. It ranges from one to six, with six being the most water efficient. Using appliances with a three-star rating, or more stars where possible, saves water.

Fixing leaks

One of the simplest ways to conserve water is to fix any leaks in pipelines, including irrigation pipelines, which transport huge amounts of water, and those in our homes. Dripping taps should also be fixed. A slowly dripping tap can waste around 20,000 litres of water a year.

REDUCING EVAPORATION

Many areas of Australia lose more than one metre of their water reserves to evaporation, while in some areas the figure may be up to three metres. This represents a significant loss of water to the atmosphere that could be used on the ground. At dams and weirs, evaporation can be reduced by covering the surface of the water with a special protective cloth or by shading it from the sun; for example, by planting large trees around the perimeter. Building deeper dams is useful – with less surface exposed to the sun, less water will evaporate. Of these ways to reduce evaporation, covering the water surface is the most problematic, as this can make the water stale and negatively affect aquatic life.

TECHNOLOGY AND WATER

Australian water suppliers are using the latest technology to improve our water efficiency. They are also looking at new ways of obtaining fresh water and saving it.

Rainwater Tanks

A water tank collects rainwater and stores it for later use. Water tanks are made from thick plastic, concrete or steel, and can be attached to the side of a house, incorporated into the garden, or even buried underground. They are hooked up to the pipes in a house. A large tank, holding up to 30,000 litres, will provide enough water for a household for a year.

The Composting Toilet

The composting toilet is not a new idea, but it has experienced renewed interest in recent years due to the large reduction in water usage that it can obtain. A normal toilet uses up to six litres for each flush, whereas a composting toilet uses no water at all. Instead it breaks down the waste material in an air- and water-tight container, eventually producing compost that can be used on the garden. Although composting toilets require a little more work, they can save many thousands of litres of water a year.

COMPUTERISED MONITORING

We now have sophisticated monitoring systems for our major dams and weirs. These provide information on potential flooding, leaks and other disturbances that may result in changes in the water supply. They also help detect problems early and reduce the possibility of water wastage.

REDUCING WATER WASTAGE

The Infrastructure Leakage Index allows water suppliers to reduce the amount of water wasted during normal supply. It calculates major water losses, such as leaking pipes. Water meters are not able to do this; they measure only how much water is used. Another important invention is the tensiometer, a device that measures moisture levels in soil, allowing farmers to determine more precisely how much water their crops require. Drip-feed irrigation systems have dramatically reduced the amount of water used to grow crops. Water is dripped directly into the soil around each plant, reducing both the amount of water wasted and the amount lost to evaporation.

Perth Sea Water Desalination Plant

In late 2006, Australia's first large scale desalination plant began supplying Perth with drinking water. The water is sourced from the Indian Ocean and after being processed through the reverse osmosis method, it is sent through pipelines to households and businesses. The plant produces an average of 130 million litres of water per day and supplies around 17 per cent of Perth's drinking water. To reduce its environmental impact, the plant is powered by electricity from a wind farm near the city.

FAST FACT

CYPRUS, AN ISLAND IN THE MEDITERRANEAN SEA, HAS SO FEW NATURAL WATER RESOURCES THAT MORE THAN THREE-QUARTERS OF ITS WATER SUPPLY COMES FROM DESALINATION.

DESALINATION

Desalination is the process of removing salt and other solids from seawater in order to produce fresh water. In many places where fresh water is scarce, such as the Middle East, desalination plants provide people with their daily water. There are two main methods of desalination. The first is called distillation and involves heating salt water to produce steam, then capturing the steam and allowing it to cool. Salt does not turn into steam, so the cooled steam, or water, has a very low salt content. The other method is called reverse osmosis. It involves pushing salt water through a very fine filter that traps the salt on one side while allowing the water to move through. Desalination plants must be located on the coastline, where they have access to plenty of seawater. In Australia, a number of desalination plants are either in operation or under construction. Perth have a desalination plant and is considering building more. Sydney has a desalination plant and Adelaide, the Gold Coast and Melbourne are all looking into constructing desalination plants.

RECYCLING WATER

There are many ways in which we can recycle the water we use in our houses and in industry. Depending on the methods used, recycled water can be used for everything from flushing the toilet to drinking!

Grey Water Recycling at Home

Grey water can be reused in many areas throughout the home, drastically reducing the need for fresh water. For example, you can use a bucket in the shower to catch excess water, which you can use on the garden. However, grey water should never be used for drinking or put on the leaves of edible plants such as vegetables and herbs, as it can contain harmful bacteria. It is important to use only biodegradable soaps and detergents at home - otherwise the chemicals in these products may contaminate the soil and kill plants.

WASTE WATER RECYCLING

Each town and city has a system of pipelines, known as a sewer, which takes wastewater away from households. Water that has been used in showers, baths and washing machines is called grey water. It contains residue from soaps and detergents. Black water is the name for water that has flushed through the toilet. It contains various contaminants. Both grey water and black water must be treated before being released into waterways. Sewage treatment plants clean the water. Water passes through a series of lagoons, where bacteria break down the solids it contains. Eventually, the water is clean enough to be released into the ocean or reused for irrigation of crops or to water parklands.

SEPTIC SYSTEMS

Rural or very isolated towns of homes may not have modern sewage systems. Instead, each house or business has a septic tank, which stores wastewater and breaks down the waste matter it contains. The water needs to be piped out occasionally and the sludge needs to be cleared out every five to eight years.

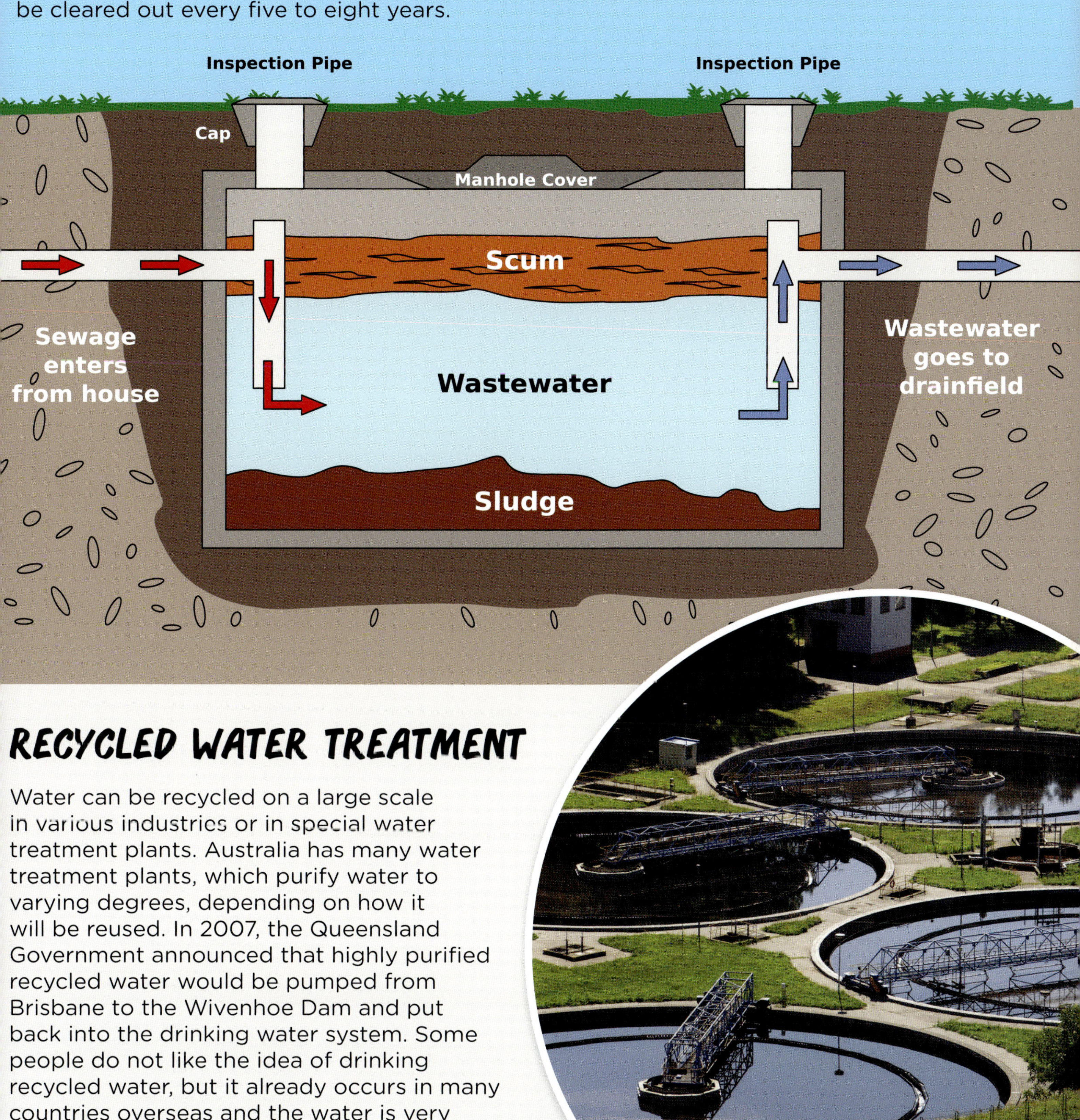

RECYCLED WATER TREATMENT

Water can be recycled on a large scale in various industries or in special water treatment plants. Australia has many water treatment plants, which purify water to varying degrees, depending on how it will be reused. In 2007, the Queensland Government announced that highly purified recycled water would be pumped from Brisbane to the Wivenhoe Dam and put back into the drinking water system. Some people do not like the idea of drinking recycled water, but it already occurs in many countries overseas and the water is very safe if it is treated properly.

WATER POLLUTION

Many human activities create water pollution. Sewage from toilets and wastewater from factories are sometimes dumped into rivers and the sea. Water from agriculture also flows back into the water system. It may contain fertilisers and other nutrients, such as nitrogen and phosphorus, which build up in rivers and dams and negatively affect plant and animal life. Wind and air currents can also spread chemicals from land to water sources.

Water pollution contaminates supplies of both fresh water and salt water. The water must go through an expensive cleaning and recycling process to make it safe for human use. In poorer countries where this is not possible, the only water people have access to may be extremely polluted, causing diseases and even death.

Litter

Litter is a common source of water pollution in Australia. However, like air pollution, water pollution can also be invisible. Rivers, lakes and streams may look dirty, but that does not mean they are polluted, as there may simply be suspended solids (like mud or silt) that need to settle. The reverse is also true; just because a waterway looks clean does not mean that it does not contain toxins that can be dangerous to human, animal and plant life.

Physical pollutants, mostly litter including plastic bags, bottles, cans and even shopping trolleys, are highly visible forms of water pollution. When it rains, litter dropped in the streets is often carried into stormwater drains that commonly lead to nearby waterways.

Litter not only makes waterways look ugly, but it can also affect water quality. It can block out sunlight and reduce the water's ability to produce oxygen which is vital for the survival of plants and animals alike. Fish, birds and other animals can also get caught in litter and be seriously injured or killed.

CHEMICALS AND BACTERIA

Chemical pollutants can affect the amount of oxygen in a waterway, kill nutrients in the water or even change the colour, taste or temperature of a waterway. This can alter the water to favour certain animal and plant species, or it can have the effect of poisoning the entire waterway and everything in it.

Bacterial pollution, coming from poor sanitation or from untreated sewage released into waterways, can spread very quickly. This can cause serious diseases in those who drink the water or bathe in it. Contaminated water is a significant problem in many developing countries. A bacteria known as 'blue-green algae' can also cause problems, making it unsuitable for livestock or humans to drink.

GROUNDWATER POLLUTION

Groundwater, which is the name given to water flowing deep below Earth's surface, exists underneath many parts of Australia. It can become polluted from a variety of sources. Toxins in soil, particularly near landfill, toxic waste sites or sewage treatment plants, can drift down into groundwater. Fertiliser and animal manure can also end up in groundwater. The water may travel long distances over time, taking pollution to larger water sources such as lakes, rivers or even the ocean.

YOU AND ME

The average Australian household uses around 200 litres of water a day. However, only 10 litres of that is for basic survival needs, such as drinking and food preparation. Australia has so few water supplies that we all need to look at how we can reduce our water usage. Here are some suggestions.

Water-Efficient Showerheads

Most standard showerheads use around 20 litres of water a minute, whereas a water-efficient showerhead uses only 7 to 9 litres a minute. By switching to a water-efficient showerhead, you can save more than 30,000 litres of water a year if you take the average 7-minute shower. By reducing your shower time, you save even more water. Putting an egg-timer in the shower is a great way to remind you when it is time to get out.

IN THE BATHROOM

At least 40 per cent of water used in the average home is used in the bathroom. An old-style single-flush toilet can consume around 11 litres of water every time you flush. Modern dual-flush systems are far more economical, using 6 litres for a full flush and only 3 litres for a half-flush. It is important to use the half-flush button as much as possible. If you have an old toilet, you can install your own water-saving device by filling a few water bottles and putting them in the cistern (the bit at the top of the toilet that holds the water). This reduces the amount of flushable water in the cistern. If you are up to the challenge, do not flush unless you really have to - you save at least 3 litres of water each time you let the yellow stuff mellow in the bowl!

OUTDOORS

Use recycled water to wash the car, rather than the hose, or take the car to a commercial car wash that uses recycled water. Native plants are great in the garden because they need far less water than non-natives and they provide a habitat for native animals. We also tend to water our gardens far more than necessary, so find out exactly how much water your plants need and stick to that amount. To reduce the loss of water through **evaporation**, watering should be done first thing in the morning or at night. Rainwater can often be channelled directly from the gutters around the roof to the garden.

IN THE KITCHEN

About 10 per cent of household water is used in the kitchen. A great deal of water gets wasted in the kitchen sink when we run the taps to wash our hands, clean vegetables or rinse dishes. To avoid this, put a plug in the sink or buy a cheap plastic tub that fits into the sink. The rinsing water can then be used on the garden, as long as you use it within 24 hours.

Top tips to reduce your water usage:

1. *Use the half-flush button on the toilet as much as possible*
2. *Make sure you have a water-efficient showerhead*
3. *Reduce your shower time*
4. *Do not run tap while brushing your teeth*
5. *Place a container in the sink when washing fruit and vegetables and use the leftover water on the garden*
6. *Fill a bucket with excess shower water, and use it on the garden*

MEASUREMENTS

LITRE
the volume of water in a cubic decimetre

KILOLITRE
1,000 litres or 1 cubic metre of water

MEGALITRE
1 million litres or 1 thousand cubic metres of water

GIGALITRE
1 thousand million litres of water

GLOSSARY

arid - dry, like a desert, with very low rainfall.

atmosphere - the cloud of gases that surrounds the Earth and protects us from ultraviolet radiation from the sun, while also trapping some sunlight and making the planet suitable for life.

black water - water that has flushed through the toilet.

bore - a large hole made down into the ground to tap into groundwater.

climate - the average weather conditions over a long period of time.

climate change - the process by which the overall temperature moves from one average to a new average.

cloud - a collection of tiny water droplets or ice crystals that have grouped together and are floating in the air.

desalination - the process of removing salt and other solids from sea water in order to produce fresh water.

distillation - a method of removing salt and other impurities from water that involves heating the water to produce steam and then capturing the steam and allowing it to cool, to become water again.

drought - a long period of little or no rainfall.

electricity - a form of energy that results from the movement of charged particles called electrons and protons.

El Niño - a cycle of warming of the surface waters along the eastern Pacific Ocean, which has a major impact on the weather, causing drought conditions in Australia.

embodied water - the amount of water it takes to produce a good or service; it is also referred to as virtual water.

evaporation - the process by which water becomes vapour

grey water - household water that has been used in showers, baths and washing machines.

groundwater - the water that is found beneath the surface of the land.

horticulture - fruit and vegetable farming.

hydro-electricity - energy that uses the power of moving water to generate electricity.

Irrigation - extra watering above and beyond rainfall.

La Niña - the opposite weather pattern to El Niño, which often causes more flooding and wet conditions in Australia.

reverse osmosis - a method of desalination and water purifying that pushes the water through a very fine filter, which traps the salt or contaminants on one side and allows the fresh water to move through.

runoff - rainfall water that flows across the land and does not sink into the ground or evaporate.

salinity - the accumulation of salt in soil, water and groundwater.

sewage - wastewater from households that is transported through the sewer system for treatment.

sewer - the system of pipes that carries wastewater from households to treatment plants.

transpiration - the process by which leaves of plants release the water they have absorbed from rainfall and groundwater as vapour into the atmosphere.

water vapour - water in a gaseous state in the atmosphere, which is a part of the water cycle.

weir - a barrier across a river or stream that is used to collect water and prevent it from going downriver.

INDEX